TIME CONTROL
How to Stop Time Destroyers, Eliminate
Procrastination, Create an Effective Schedule and
Reclaim Your Life

JUSTIN BYERS

Time Control: How to Stop Time Destroyers, Eliminate Procrastination, Create an Effective Schedule and Reclaim Your Life

Justin Byers

Table of Contents

Introduction

It is almost a truism to rue that there are not enough hours in any given day. Each of us is constantly beset by a range of seemingly conflicting impulses and desires. If we work full days, the challenge to infuse the remaining handful of moments outside of work with value is a daunting one. How do we stay healthy, active, and manage to constantly enrich our personal lives while providing for ourselves and our loved ones simultaneously?

It seems under this admittedly intense pressure, something simply must give. If children need to be at school by seven, and work starts at nine, there seems no hope of increasing our own personal productivity—especially when we are completely drained of resources by the end of the day. How many of us come home, for example, and feel exhilarated at the opportunity to clean and organize a garage, or perhaps manage a number of correspondences that have piled up after a few days?

This is no small challenge for any of us. It's not that there are "winners" and "losers" in life—it's not that certain people just have a magical ability to accomplish whatever they set out to do. Everything worth doing and achieving in life takes courage, dedication, patience, and a positive attitude. That being said, it is possible to learn ways to become more productive in your life. No one is born inherently knowing how to accomplish their largest dreams. Certainly a person here or there will figure it out on their own—these are the big successes we aspire to be—and it's possible, with a little mental adjustment and motivation, to embark on that journey. Increasing your personal productivity requires you to plan with precision, learn with purpose toward your goals, and accept temporary setbacks with grace and a playful attitude.

Very few people on this earth manage to go to sleep at night having accomplished everything they set out to do. If they have, it's a good bet they haven't aspired to complete much to begin with. Do yourself a favor now and try to remember the last time you went to bed satisfied that you'd accomplished a sizeable fraction of what you'd set out to on a given day. It may take a few moments, but try to remember a day when things went well, and perhaps only a minor task or two fell through the cracks of your best intentions.

Now consider your days in general. What is different about the day-to-day affairs of your life, and those that really shine in your mind as successes? Was it luck? Did everything just fall into place without a single hitch? Were you driven by some desire to accomplish your tasks on the better day, while remaining generally uninspired on others? Perhaps, knowing the next day would be filled to the brim with daunting chores, you made a mental schedule of everything that would happen, and stuck to it the next day.

It is possible, with practice and patience, to manage day-to-day tasks with consistently higher levels of success, given the right understanding both of what happens when we are doing things right and what happens when we are not quite so task-oriented as we ought to be.

The purpose of this book is to give you a brief but solid foundation for harnessing a wide range of knowledge and practices that can help you save substantial amounts of time throughout the day. This time adds up to minutes every hour and hours every day. By practicing the tips presented below, you can expect to experience an abundant increase in productivity, and you will even find that these positive changes beget themselves in a self-encouraging fashion. Moreover, you'll discover this in less time than one can imagine.

Ending the day positively and successfully is a wonderful feeling, and will promote the same attitude and sense of direction in the next day, and the next, and so on. After all, how appealing does it sound to you to begin every day with a set plan of action, a method for avoiding hang-ups along the way, and an overall sense of how one day's productivity will enhance the next? The amount of time saved in a given day can invariably be used in turn to enrich the quality of your life and the lives of your loved ones.

This book is roughly divided into two sections. The first section is devoted to identifying goals and fostering a productive schedule by eliminating unnecessary wastes of time and energy. You will need all you can get of both, and as you'll see shortly, there are ways to free up hours, minutes, and even seconds of your day to harness towards personal productivity. The second section focuses on ways of motivating and energizing yourself in the most productive ways possible. Subjects are loosely grouped together so that related topics will be covered one after the other, in order to provide you with a more intuitive understanding of the points being made.

Increasing your personal productivity represents a commitment, and the more you want out of life, the more you'll have to commit to this change. All the tips, insights, and suggestions in this book won't do a person any good if he or she is unwilling to follow through with making real changes to his or her life. Much of the advice is practical and represents a wealth of knowledge that simply gets overlooked or forgotten in the day-to-day bustle.

A good example of something about productivity that we may not realize *we know*: we begin most new and engaging tasks with a burst of enthusiasm and productivity. Anywhere from a fifth to a third of the way through, we begin to feel as though we are too far away from our objective to possibly be successful. Suddenly, halfway through, we find ourselves reinvigorated and determined to finish, brimming with new insights and ideas. Another ten percent of the task gets completed, however, and suddenly we feel as though we are farther away from reaching the goal than we ever were. We struggle and scramble for progress until we are around ninety percent complete with the task. With the end in sight, the completion of whatever we set out to accomplish seems inevitable, and almost effortless. This is true of almost anything we set out to achieve, regardless if it is a marathon, learning to play a musical instrument, or writing a novel. Somehow, we humans go through the same meta-procedures in the acquisition of new tasks, regardless of what the task may actually entail. Knowing this can prevent you from turning away from your goals. If you find yourself feeling stuck after about a third of a large goal, *good*! That's how you're supposed to feel. With that in mind, why not keep going with it and see what happens next?

Again, there's nothing innate or inherent about the ability of furthering our own productivity. Everyone who manages to accomplish great things does so by following the same essential set of rules and guidelines. They understand the principle of motivational processing outlined above. They have trained themselves to forgo a large number of leisurely activities that eat up time disproportionate to the amount of fulfillment they can provide. They accept setbacks and errors as opportunities for learning and personal growth, and they do not accept failure. They know what they want, and they are unswerving in their determination to get it. Knowing how the minds and techniques of productive individuals work can allow us to mimic their ways and obtain our own goals.

How to Free Up Time

Make Sure to Get it in Writing

Highly productive individuals know what they want, and they've very likely got it written down somewhere. This habit cannot be stressed enough. It is far too easy for us to become sidetracked if we haven't clearly identified for ourselves precisely what we are planning to accomplish.

Identify what it is you want out of life that you don't presently have. It could be anything—more money, better organization, healthier living, better personal relationships, and so on. Now, with that in mind, recognize that anything additional you want in your life requires first and foremost a change in the way that you already do things. You'll need to free up time here and there. You'll also need to make an effort to complete whatever activity you've selected, and generally take note of your progress along the way.

Take careful note of things you've completed successfully in the past. You may not be surprised to learn that you've done similar or related tasks many, many times before you set out to accomplish something larger. Think about the times that you have done so and come up with several reasons you made any specific change to your life. Write them down somewhere, in a notebook or on a computer—you'll be coming back to these. Also, write down whatever it is you decided you want more of from your time on earth.

Avoid the pitfall of deciding you want something like more money just because you can't think of anything else to want. Be totally honest with yourself, and go for broke. If money is something you want more of, and it probably is, run with that. But does something else interest you more? Is there a talent you wish to acquire? A sport you wish to take up? Do you want to go back to school? Ask yourself what sort of person you want to be, and what sort of accomplishments that person can achieve.

Avoiding Displeasure Vs. Actively Seeking Pleasure

Most of the things you've probably written down are things that you want to gravitate *towards*. Many of you will have written things like "a new house" or "a better paying job" or "a higher golf score." Now comes the part where you consider what motivated you to do similar things in the past. An overwhelming section of the population does not make significant changes in order to move towards positive goals. That is to say, most of us don't make an attempt to do something because it's what we *want* to do. Instead, we usually move away from things that we *don't want*—we try to avoid negative consequences. The reasons for this most common decision-making process are unclear, but think of the task of losing weight. It's most common that people begin engaging in healthier practices not in order to improve an already stellar constitution, but rather because they are trying to avoid being perceived as unpleasant looking by themselves or others. Or they lose weight because they were instructed to by their care provider.

This way of making decisions and allotting time—avoiding displeasure as opposed to actively seeking pleasure—is not by any means an inferior outlook on life. How could it be, if so many of us adopt this point of view? When seeking new undertakings, especially something like increasing your own personal productivity, it's a great idea to identify the things that can go wrong—and things will, from time to time. The first thing to establish is the "why" of what you are attempting to do. Are you one of the few who easily gravitates towards new tasks and personal goals with ease? If so, when you visualize yourself obtaining new skills or completing objectives you've established, you will experience a much greater ease in appreciating the results. If you tend to avoid displeasure, you will need to come up with goals and objectives that emphasize the fact that you wish to move away from something that is presently bothering you.

In this case, something like "new home" will need to be rephrased into "better living situation." This is because an idea like "new home" will invariably come weighted with stress and unpleasant possibilities. If you are geared to avoid unpleasantness, it's always a good idea to emphasize any discomfort you are presently feeling. Get fed up. Don't get fed up with yourself, or with others (unless it will genuinely benefit you to do so), but get fed up at situations, things that you do out of sheer habit, or perhaps even that your present circumstances aren't as bright as you deserve. Use that energy to make something happen about it. As time progresses and you get more successes under your belt, you'll naturally begin to gravitate towards new objectives as opposed to avoiding unpleasant situations. Since you'll become more familiar with positive outcomes, you'll be more familiar with the positive feelings they inherently elicit. Eventually, you'll be forward-oriented in the accomplishment of your goals, confident in the knowledge that your work and determination is getting you somewhere.

The secret to identifying goals in this fashion involves turning the unpleasant situation or possibility into something to strive for. If you are the type of person who tries to avoid displeasure and undesirable circumstances, you have a great arsenal of motivation at your disposal. For example, if someone at work or in your social circle behaves in a way that you find unacceptable, you suddenly have a concrete and obtainable goal right in front of you. Why not, in this case, set a goal for yourself to deal with this person in a way that will remove the problem in a fair and beneficial way? If you find yourself constantly plagued by stiff limbs or a sore back, why not set a goal to find a way to eliminate this discomfort? *With a minimal amount of thought, you can turn anything you wish to avoid into a goal you wish to achieve*. This is really the same thing as identifying things that we want, it just takes a slight modification and we have something positive to strive for.

Motivated and productive people are incredibly skilled at avoiding time-wasting activities, whatever they may be. It's impossible to increase your personal productivity while keeping the basic structure of your day the same. This restructuring of your routine must consist of identifying and eliminating activities that do not progress your goals. This end requires discipline and sometimes may require significant adjustment, but there's no way around the process of freeing up more time to be productive if that's really what you want.

Managing Time Destroyers

Listed below are several things that greatly hinder our personal productivity on a regular basis. Each of these elements shares a great deal in common with the next, and all of them are forms of wasting time. As you read each section, keep a lookout for things that you do personally, and make note of how you might eliminate the unwanted habit or activity.

Procrastination

The bane of productivity. Procrastination is so commonplace that many of us are accustomed to putting off tasks or chores almost without noticing we do so. Any challenge or chore we are loath to commit our personal time to is likely to be put off for as long as possible, if not indefinitely. In the short term, procrastination is a nuisance to ourselves and those that depend on us. But unfortunately, that is as far as most of us care to consider it. There is a much deeper, more insidious reality at stake when we put off either day-to-day tasks or personal dreams of accomplishment.

If we're of the state of mind that puts off cleaning and organizing things for as long as possible, suddenly we're in the midst of an almost insurmountable heap of disorganization. This accumulation of disorder is actually quite damaging to our psyches, and those of us who tend to be on the messy side can easily be discouraged by how much messier things get when we don't attend to them directly. This fact is well-understood by organized people, and in fact they often remark with confusion about how their less-clean friends manage to let things go so far.

If you want to learn how to play a musical instrument, draw, draft, or develop any other skill, procrastination can have devastating consequences in the long-term if not properly addressed. It has been known to psychologists and other health-care professionals for decades that as we approach the ends of our lives, we regret the things we haven't managed. Our reflections are not filled with remorse at the things we managed to accomplish, but the things we never set out to do in the first place. The leading cause of these unachieved goals? They were put off indefinitely. For whatever reason, the motivation to do something about accomplishing them never set in.

You owe it to yourself to limit these regrets as much as humanly possible, and it is very possible to do so. Procrastination generally sets in because we want to avoid the displeasure of completing a task (note your personality type!) and possible failure. When we visualize completing tasks that we are likely to lead us into a spell of procrastination, we may feel a vague anxiety about engaging in the activity. Though vague, it is a powerfully motivating force—suddenly we are willing to do anything else but the task we just imagined doing. If the task has a deadline, it grows nearer and nearer until we're forced to do a frenzied and slipshod job. This often leads to failure, which in turn reinforces the idea that the task is unpleasant to begin with. The next time you are faced with such a task, you experience the same feelings of dread.

It's a funny quirk of human nature that we often do a poor job due to self-imposed time-restraints (the result of procrastination), and yet proceed to blame it on some inherent failure. Who doesn't recall powering through a term paper the night before it's due? We may even be consciously aware that we could have done a much better job if we only hadn't avoided the task, yet we *still* manage to take the failure personally. We then allow it to inhibit our productivity in the future. In order to overcome procrastination, we first have to separate our actions and mistakes from ourselves.

Managing Tasks with Optimism

To begin with, it's a good idea to take a look at the difference between optimism and pessimism. We'll see the role this plays in procrastination almost immediately. Say, for instance, that you've reached the extent of your professional career and need to undertake new courses or perhaps earn a higher degree in order to advance. A pessimist will take one look at the course requirements and time commitments needed to accomplish this goal and bemoan his fate. A commitment of two years or more under a rigorous academic routine seems impossible. A pessimist sees all of this discomfort and stress at once and backs away.

Now, to the pessimist, it might seem like the opposite person would simply charge forward and take on everything at once without hesitation. Optimists do, after all, seem to maintain an incredible can-do attitude, even in the face of incredible stress. But the reality of an optimistic point of view is really more subtle than that.

An optimist doesn't see the same challenge as a pessimist—in this case, a positive thinker doesn't immediately retreat from academic advancement because the entirety of it seems impossible. An optimist will face such an incredible task by breaking it down into steps. They recognize that just because the energy that must be spent entering and taking new courses will be massive, it won't be all at once, and can be done in steps.

In other words, the first thing that comes into the mind of an optimist needn't be—and in fact, probably isn't—*"I can do this, no problem!"* Instead, it is far more likely something like—*"So, how do I break this down into manageable steps?"* The optimist makes sure the next step is something he or she can integrate into life, while the pessimist becomes overwhelmed by all the steps at once. This simple yet subtle skill of breaking down colossal responsibilities into discreet and manageable steps is vital to increasing your own productivity. Every big dream you have can be accomplished by breaking that dream down into several dozen or perhaps even a hundred smaller and discreet stages. These stages form the foundation of the dream becoming your reality.

Overcoming Large Tasks

Try this simple way of managing your thoughts the next time you are faced with what appears to be a large task: ask yourself what the very first thing you need to do in order to accomplish it is, then set to doing that without paying attention to the larger goal. Nothing that requires long periods of time ever needs to be accomplished at once, so why should we allow ourselves to feel all of the accompanying stress at the outset? By making the practice of dealing with tasks in smaller chunks a habit, we can vastly increase our productivity—maybe the optimist winds up in school for another couple of years, for example, but when time for advancement comes, the pessimist has not done the work because they have found it too daunting.

Procrastination can also come in the opposite form, however. Perhaps you've found the perfect way to manage those huge tasks in life, but little ones—doing laundry or mowing the lawn—manage to slip away from you constantly. Here, the procrastinator likely doesn't feel particularly overwhelmed by the chore. Rather, it may be seen as a nuisance or something unnecessary when all is said and done. A person who despises the sound of the vacuum—let's face it, even the most modern earplugs can't do much good against that noise—will not avoid vacuuming out of being afraid of failure. Instead, he or she simply can't stand the sound and will put off doing it until an inordinate amount of dust has accumulated.

Overcoming Tasks You Despise

If this is the case, another thought experiment may be called on. Here, take something small—perhaps a weekly chore that you commonly forget to accomplish on time. Now, make the commitment to do it *far more often than you need to* in the space of one week. If you despise vacuuming, and know it should be done on a weekly basis but manage to forget it regularly enough that you (or your spouse) have a problem with it, resolve for one week to vacuum on a daily basis. *Seven times in one week.* If dust tends to accumulate on your car because you dislike getting it washed for whatever reason, wash it after work every day.

Focus on a single task in one week and commit to tackling that task far more times than you would reasonably need done. Remember, we may desire a wide range of changes to our productivity, but the rule of optimism implores us to break things down lest we become overwhelmed. You may even feel a little silly while you're doing this—that's great. Make it a game, consider it practice, and once a successful week is finished, be sure to reflect on it with playful pride. It will be far easier to remember tasks you've tackled like this than it was before.

Remember, choose *one task only*. A week-long commitment to two or more chores is less likely to be successful, since you will be far more likely to get bored, annoyed, or forgetful with several.

Procrastination has an almost ephemeral quality to it at times. Often, we just need to *do it* instead of thinking about doing it. This previous exercise is meant to familiarize ourselves with the reality that a task we reflexively avoid because it is unpleasant is actually not so bad at all. There's no chore we can accomplish that is actually "difficult," but our perception of the chore can be something akin to a battle that never ends. This is often because we put off mildly unpleasant routines until they have grown daunting. A regular habit of completing simple tasks here and there is far less time-consuming. The trick is simply to stay constant in our completion of the task.

Procrastinating From... Success?

As strange as it may sound, procrastination can arise from our fear of success just as much as it can from a fear of failure. We feel that the more we accomplish, the more we will be burdened with responsibility. Here, it's up to the individual to make a decision. If you feel that you really do know you wouldn't desire the outcome of acquiring a new talent or completing something you feel important to you, ask yourself why the goal is important in the first place. If the nuisance of new responsibility really isn't worth achieving something you thought you wanted, you still won't know whether or not you can accomplish it. For many of us, it's that question that can push us forward, whatever the consequences may be. Besides, progress towards your goals is always a learning experience. It's unlikely that you'll be unable to handle any additional responsibilities afforded to you by your accomplishment, given the amount of time and resources you spent learning how to do it in the first place.

If you're unsure of exactly why you're procrastinating on a given project or task, and this will happen from time to time, sit down and identify what it is you want out of the completion of the goal. Once you've determined what you want ultimately out of a goal, take a look at things that might stand in your way. Not all resources are tangible. You might be procrastinating on a project because you don't know how to proceed with it. If this is the case, you'll need to find someone who knows how to do it and proceed from there. Breaking tasks down in this way can draw attention to areas of personal strength that we need to develop in order to make it a reality. Often times, if we can find the reasons we're putting off a task, we can address those reasons directly and then proceed far less hindered by doubt.

Time-Distortion

Another rampant productivity-eater in our society. If we're running errands, we may assume we need only an hour or so to complete, say, grocery shopping and a stop at the post-office before we pick our children up from school or grab dinner with friends. Suddenly, though, we're stuck in traffic, and after two-and-a-half hours, we arrive at the post-office to find a long line stretched out before us. We've misjudged the amount of time it should take to complete tasks, typically by misjudging the amount of time it will take simply to travel from one place to the next.

We can also lose time rapidly in our own minds. We might sit ourselves down with the intention of doing something, but become easily distracted (especially in front of a computer with internet access) or begin daydreaming. Perhaps we engage in something other than what we'd intended to entirely. If our goals aren't clear to us, or we haven't allotted an appropriate amount of time towards their completion, we aren't using our time to its fullest. A few suggestions for combating time-distortion are listed below. Generally, they require an understanding of how we intend to use our time before we begin a given task.

There are twenty-four hours in a given day. We should be asleep for at least seven of these. With fifteen or sixteen hours remaining, it's no wonder we often wonder what happened to the day—they don't last very long to begin with, and we've got to make the most out of the time that we have. Start taking account of how long trips to the store and such related tasks actually take—you'll have a better idea of what to plan for if you can anticipate the time needed to follow through with something.

Avoiding the Rush

It's easy for people to fall into habits, especially where routes and activities are concerned. But consider the following: since most of us are likely to schedule errands after work, how much time do we save by attempting to do things *before* work?

By another token, many of us set off to accomplish things without giving due consideration to what route we should take in order to get the tasks accomplished fastest. We set about errands in piecemeal fashion and take the largest roads, which also may be the most congested and time consuming. So much of America has become accustomed to living significant portions of life in our car that we tend not to plan well for things like traffic or roadwork. If an errand must be completed two miles away, it is probably a better idea to stop oneself from automatically taking the freeway, which may be a convenient straight-line, but could also be little more than a parking lot directly after work. Make use of city maps online or GPS devices to view better possible routes to your common destinations.

Remember, it all adds up, especially if you're faced with a massive amount of things that need to be accomplished in a given day. Typically, those who beat morning traffic to their jobs spend less time in their cars and are far less stressed out at the end of the day. It's the difference between coming home after an hour or two stuck in traffic and waking up maybe a half-hour in advance to pre-empt the morning rush. In the long run, there's no question of who feels better by the end of the day. Whatever your situation, it will benefit you to find ways to avoid the hustle-and-bustle of people attempting to complete their own objectives during the busiest hours of the day.

One might raise the complaint that in order to do that, one needs to wake up far earlier in order to prepare. This is correct, and it's a valid complaint, but consider overall how much time you will be stuck in traffic or delayed *by waiting until the busiest times of the day.* True, if your errands require a trip to the bank or the DMV, the hours are far less conducive to making it before work, but another burgeoning reality plays in our favor. Many institutions that are mainly open during our own hours of professional operations have become automated, and the trend only promises to increase as the years go by.

Removing Menial Errands

If you're savvy enough, you can circumvent many menial errands in the first place by taking advantage of these automated services. Why try to visit the DMV or bank at all, for example, when what you're trying to do can probably be done without going there at all? Is it worth your time when you can accomplish the same ends without leaving your home?

Taken to extremes, accomplishing small tasks online can save massive amounts of time. Consider trips to a clothing store. While it may be best to go to one when looking at clothing for special occasions, there's far less need to go searching about in a clothing store for things if you already know what you're looking for. The initial reaction to this suggestion is generally one of disdain, but in most cases the benefits of being able to locate what you want online simply far outweighs the experience of traveling to a store where an increase in one's productivity is concerned. Why take time out of your day, for example, to take a chance on locating socks or t-shirts you enjoy wearing if you can locate them online in a fraction of the time?

The more you can do from the comfort of your home, the less time you'll have spent travelling from A to B. While it may seem counterintuitive to begin using the internet for these tasks, in the end you'll find loads of time freed up in order to pursue things of greater importance. Plus, an online trip to the bank, clothing store, and gift-shop for an upcoming birthday are all far more likely to be remembered in the short amounts of time it will take them to complete online. There is a tradeoff, to be sure, but proponents of online errand-running don't look back. It's no accident that organizations like Amazon.com and eBay have been so incredibly successful in the past few years, nor that eBook publishing is so greatly on the rise. The convenience has managed to tangibly enrich the lives of millions by freeing them of the time and hassle that was so commonplace just a small number of years ago.

Don't Forget Weekends

Your weekends count. Many people who've managed to find success in their personal goals have done so solely on weekends. This means that you'll need to take advantage of your free time Saturdays and Sundays (or whatever your weekend may be). It's surprising how many people don't count time on weekends as time to be used toward the direction of a task. Both days could be very useful for scheduling larger blocks of time towards the accomplishment of a specific goal. If you're used to taking it easy over the weekend, this can represent quite an adjustment. We tend to feel that we work hard and deserve time to relax. If this is the case for you, keep in mind that even though the typical work week lasts five days, Saturday and Sunday still count towards the number of days you have total.

Of course you can justify relaxing a few hours at a time now and then, but if you're resistant to use your weekends in a productive way, you've already forfeited nearly thirty percent of the total available time you'd have—and this time is not burdened by the responsibilities of work. Over time (and a short amount of time at that), you'll grow used to the busier schedule. It's easy for us to give ourselves too much relaxation time. It does feel nice to spend time unburdened by deadlines and responsibilities, but we can do so without going overboard.

Get More Done by Planning

We tend to go through daily affairs with a general idea of what we need to do. Getting it in writing, scheduling times, and making sure we're sticking to things as much as possible will help in the development of personal productivity.

It's too easy to forget a task here and there in order to leave something to chance on busy days. Active use of a daily or even an hourly planner will benefit anyone in countless ways—the reminders serve to ensure that we are aware we began our day with certain objectives and then to remind us of our commitment to personal productivity. Write out your schedule the night prior. Glance at it and remind yourself what needs to be done as soon as you wake up. Take note of everything you intend to do. Take the schedule with you. Provide yourself with reminders of when you should be ending one task and starting another. Give yourself breathing room here and there just in case something gets in the way.

Remember to schedule in breakfast, lunch, and dinner. This is also a good opportunity for those who wish to begin eating healthier foods. Minimal research on the internet—again, such a useful medium—can determine endless healthy meals for breakfast, lunch and dinner. If you assign yourself meal plans for the next day at the time of creating your schedule, you'll be far more likely to stick to your plan. Healthy foods will lead to healthier feelings, increased motivation and elevated mood as well.

Creating Your Daily Schedule

Most people have a schedule at work, and a vague idea of what they want to do the rest of the time. The reason that work is so dependent on scheduling is because it is an efficient way of managing time, and it's important to take this attitude with you wherever you go if you're trying to increase your efficiency and productivity. A clear schedule will help you avoid procrastination and time-distortion at once, since it will bestow upon you a delineated blueprint towards achieving your objectives. Start with when you plan to wake up in the morning, and finish with when you plan to go to sleep. It is especially important to establish a bedtime, as doing so will help you fall asleep and wake up more easily.

Daily schedules can provide the impetus to accomplish many tasks, but even with such an itinerary, it's still important to identify things that we gravitate towards in life. We all possess far more goals, regardless of how vague or undefined they might be, than we possess time to accomplish them. As with procrastination in general, we may simply stick to the basics—work, family, friends—and let the overwhelming objective of collecting enough motivation to follow through with the acquisition of a new talent fall to the wayside. The difficulty here is, that since we have not identified what specifically we set out to accomplish, we accomplish very little if anything at all.

What You Think You Can Do vs. What You Really Do

It won't be uncommon, especially at the beginning, to experience a massive disparity between what we think we can accomplish in one day and what actually gets done. This is even truer for people with families, who may suddenly be called to assist a son or daughter unexpectedly. If this happens, give yourself a more modest schedule the next day and try again. As you get better at completing goals in the time you've given yourself, you can slowly add more to your schedule.

Many people set out with twelve or thirteen things that they want to accomplish in a given day, only to find that perhaps as few as four were actually feasible. This is to be expected in the beginning, and in many ways it is the direct opposite of wondering where all the time in our day went. With a schedule written out, one can make notes regarding completion or progress of something, and save them over time. It is always beneficial to go back and see what has actually been done in a day's or week's time to determine a more realistic sense of what can be accomplished in those spans.

Scheduling Minor Tasks

Try this exercise: Write down three to five things you wish to accomplish within the next week or so. These are most likely simple tasks—calling a family member you haven't spoken to in a while, or practicing a new dinner recipe you got from a friend, for example. Their completion should not be terribly time-consuming, and perhaps it may not ultimately matter if the deed is ever in fact completed. The important thing is to come up with things that you perceive would benefit your life. Whatever chores or activities you choose, write them down before you've written your schedule for the next day. Think of ways to incorporate one small goal into your schedule, but for now, try your best to leave time open. You'll see why at the end of this exercise.

Ultimately you'll try to include each of these small goals into your daily affairs until you've run out—you won't always have time for these things, and that's okay—that's an unavoidable fact of life. However, if you do incorporate something into your schedule, make sure you actually have the time and resources to complete it. If you don't, try not to be too harsh on yourself for not accomplishing it, especially when you first begin writing a schedule like this one. At the outset, shoot for accomplishing one or two of these goals every couple of days. Again, they should take no more than an hour to complete. These simple goals will also help you build confidence towards larger ones.

We tend to focus on the end result of our goals rather than the process we'll need to take in order to achieve them. We know what we want, which is a good start, but the emphasis of any goal needs to be shifted towards the way in which we make it a reality. Where we're going is one thing, but we need to have a plan to get there. It's important to think about how we move towards these goals. It is equally important to gather as much information as we need in order to proceed with them. To this end, it will always be helpful to search for additional information on the subjects wherever we may find it.

It's astounding, for example, how many aspiring novelists will forgo an important step in the process: *reading other novelists.* Successful writers are habitual readers, and they are so adept at doing so that they can unconsciously absorb information about pacing, structure, and scene-writing by looking at other people's work. A writer who reads less than an hour a day is tantamount to an athlete who leaves out the basics of his or her training.

Whatever you decide to do, be sure to keep up with whoever else is doing it, and what they are doing. Minor goals are a way of experimenting with this feeling of self-accomplishment and allowing it to bolster your resolve toward larger ones.

As you progress toward whatever minor goals you've set out for yourself, make an effort to derive enjoyment from the process itself. No doubt there will be times when you are frustrated in your progress, or unable to complete something you'd wanted to, but this frustration is only temporary, and you can always try again tomorrow. What will be permanent is the sense of accomplishment you receive throughout your productivity. Realize that whatever you do, you are bringing yourself closer to your ultimate goal.

Scheduling Moderate Tasks

Once you've written down minor goals, try to identify moderate ones. These are somewhat trickier to identify, but they may include organizing a portion of your home, arranging a family vacation, or even reading a book series if that accomplishment is important enough to you. These goals can take anywhere from a week to several months to complete. As with your minor goals, try to include them on a regular basis, but unlike minor goals, these will require you to break them down into smaller sections.

Be prepared to be more flexible in terms of planning the completion of your moderate goals. They are often things we've never done before, and may require constant adjustments as we plot our course to their termination. This may take some time and patience to get used to, as the completion of minor goals is simple by comparison. For the most part, we complete them or not. Moderate goals are commonly abandoned mid-completion because the steps suddenly become obscure or we are somehow distracted from our original purpose.

How many times have we begun something and continued with it for a week or two only to become overwhelmed by the necessities of dealing with immediate problems? This happens, and it may be rare to resume our previous intentions because we have fallen out of whatever rhythm we'd established. The trick is to remind ourselves—again, the schedule comes in handy. While we may not remember what we'd wished to accomplish, it will still be written down amongst the goals and schedules we've saved. This will greatly assist you in picking up where you left off.

Scheduling Your Big Goals in Life

Once you've identified a moderate goal or two, think of all the big things in life you would like to accomplish. These might include learning a foreign language, obtaining a new professional credential or degree, or even writing a novel. These goals will almost invariably take over a year to complete, sometimes more than ten. Unlike moderate goals, they will not be difficult to identify within you, because they represent some of your highest aspirations. However, it can be even more vague and unclear how to complete these tasks. These are big dreams, and they are often scary to think about. It's no small wonder why. Major goals represent major investments of time and energy, and the prospect of failure looms like a grand shadow next to the aspirations. Those of us who speak English as our native language may shudder at the thought of someday traveling to a foreign country without a guide or translator. If you wish to write a novel, you might tremble to learn that the average amount of rejections faced by a writer's first novel presently hovers around sixty, and rises steadily each year.

Nowhere more than in the case of major goals do we possess the tendency to let our fear paralyze our productivity. Human beings often go their entire lives without attempting such dire tasks in earnest, and this is fine, if you don't feel that you are worthy of success. Any task may appear extraordinarily difficult to complete, but it will be impossible to complete if it is never attempted. In fact, it will become clearer to you as you progress in your own quest towards higher levels of productivity that much of what we accomplish is achieved only because we made the conscious and self-directed attempt to do so in the first place.

If such tasks as major goals were easy to accomplish, they would be far less valuable in the measure of pride and self-esteem they can afford us upon their completion. In fact, if you have embarked upon the completion of a major goal in the past, you may have experienced a huge burst of creative productivity in the beginning. This feeling is just as common as the experience of having the wind taken out of our sails just as suddenly. This experience should not serve to dissuade you in the least—rather, try to look at it instead as a learning opportunity. You may feel exhausted or fed up with the task at hand, but as you gently urge yourself forward, consider that this is the experience everyone has while making progress in any area of their life.

Allow yourself to remain free of judgment and try to stay playful with your major goals as you progress. Remember that anything accomplished is by that very fact set apart from idle dreams that most people never attempt. Here more than anywhere, we need to foster the ability to pump ourselves up and push through the difficulties. This is where the general sense of accomplishment derived from minor and moderate goals will help us—productivity begets a productive mindset, not the other way around. If we're growing more accustomed to achieving what we need to achieve, we'll be more inclined to take on the big stuff in life.

It is important during the assembly of your schedule that you pay careful attention to what you actually need to accomplish. If something doesn't actually add to your productivity, don't include it on your schedule. This doesn't mean not to relax—there are simply more "productive" ways to do so. Identifying and eliminating things from your daily routine that suck time away from an otherwise a productive itinerary is a good way to free up yet more time for you to do what you need to do.

Take Advantage of Your Peak Productivity Times

Pay attention to when you are most productive. Much of the material in this book suggests working early and quickly, but everyone's cycle of productivity is different. While it's true that a majority of people will more greatly benefit from tackling tasks in the morning, there are plenty of people who swear by evening productivity, and if that really turns out to be the case for you, then focus on major and important goals during those hours and do menial and minor tasks when you are at your least productive. To establish your times of peak productivity, it might be useful to keep up a reverse schedule, that is to say keep track of what you're doing and write it down every hour or so. You might be surprised to find after several days of this that you tend to be incredibly productive during certain periods of the day, and it's a good idea to take advantage of those times.

While most goals will either be accomplished or put off to another date, some goals might require more precise systems of measurement than time. Say, for instance, that you want to spend more time developing your blog. If you give yourself two hours a day to develop your blog, but only write a hundred or so words in that time-frame, you've done far less work on the blog than the work would actually imply. Give yourself a word-count or other milestone, say 1,000 words or an entire article. That way you're not just staring at the screen for most of the time, since you'll be more motivated to reach the word count or completion of the article than you would be just waiting out the clock. In some cases, we have to forgo time-restraints in lieu of more substantial accomplishments to ensure that we are using our time as wisely as possible.

A person who commits to write or work "for an hour" hasn't really committed to anything substantial. A person who commits to do the same, but also comes up with a word-count or more discreet measure of progress has provided an additional motivational cue, and will accomplish far more overall. You'll find that establishing set amounts of work you wish to complete in this fashion will keep you moving far quicker than would otherwise be feasible.

Scheduling Minor, Moderate and Major Goals

Next comes incorporating minor, moderate, and major goals into your daily schedule. These goals should be clearly stated, with the expected outcomes stated in a way that you will know whether or not you've accomplished that goal. You'll be able to leave out the more specific details as you grow accustomed to knowing your own expectations and work capacities. The initial note-taking is not to keep track of what you are failing to accomplish, but rather to give you a clear sense of what you are trying to do, so remember to stay an optimist and focus on the fact that you are trying. It's okay to modify and scale back your goals if you constantly find yourself coming short of them. Indeed, if you're constantly falling short of your expectations, you should take it down a notch or two. Consistently not reaching your daily goals is not a reflection of your capabilities, but rather an indication that you're taking on too much.

For starters, minor goals should be present in daily affairs perhaps four to five times a week, depending on the length of each. Moderate goals should occur as often, but allow yourself to work on a maximum of two at a time to begin with. Major goals should be worked on as much as possible—an hour or two a day is optimal. This represents an obvious challenge to the productive individual; two hours out of any given day can be exceedingly difficult to spare. Some of the suggestions below can help to make this possible.

Eliminating Time Wasters to Add Time

First, eliminate forms of time-wasting media. These forms of entertainment can be responsible for more time-distortion than anything else. The average American watches five hours of television a day. However, if you ask the average American how much time he or she *spends watching television*, he may answer along the lines of "I barely watch TV."

Both realities can't be true, and here's what happens: we get home from work and flip on the television before we eat dinner. We're not consciously aware that it's on, but it nevertheless remains a constant distractor until it is time for us to go to sleep. Maybe we attempted to do something else while the television was on, but we were far less efficient because we were continuously distracted by the television screen. We may also not count movies as watching television for some reason, as if watching movies doesn't cut into the amount of time we have in a given day just as much as television does. If you're unsure of how much television you watch on a regular basis, make an effort to jot down times during the day that the television is on, when it is turned off, what shows you watch, and so on. It's true that TV can afford simple and immediate entertainment, but consider the very real possibility that it cuts into your productivity in a very severe way.

The internet, while cited above as a major source of time-saving resources, can have an even more devastating effect on one's personal productivity. Not long ago, the game *FarmVille* on Facebook surged to prominence and was featured all across the country as an instant and pervasive fad across the nation. People began setting their alarm clocks according to the seeds they had planted in the virtual farm the night before, and many checked their farms constantly to ensure everything was proceeding as they had planned. The game also had a social aspect to further color its appeal; one could leave messages on neighboring farms, help get rid of pesky rodents or insects, and even leave gifts. The allure of this game was not restricted to any age group, and in fact was designed to include aspects that would appeal to a gigantic numbers of people across the world.

The end result was countless hours invested in what was essentially an *imaginary farm*. While this may have been immediately entertaining, it produced little in the way of real accomplishment. One can only wonder what would have happened if instead of a video game, people had one day waken up and gone after substantial pursuits in the same fashion.

It is important to identify sites on the internet that can waste your time. There is no end to them. Social networking sites can be excellent tools for advancing nearly any goal you wish to pursue, but without caution, one can wind up losing more time on these sites than anywhere else. It is wise to avoid the games and activities offered up by the associates of these websites—their content is designed to pull you away from what you originally felt you ought to be doing in order to invest your time (and possibly money) in menial activities. These activities produce no ultimate impact on your life other than to further impinge your valuable time and resources. If a goal is really worth achieving, these sites need to be visited sparingly and with a specific purpose.

Taking back the time that we willingly give up to television and other forms of media is often the first step in increasing productivity. Against daily demands in addition to what we'd like to accomplish, it suddenly seems difficult to justify an hour or two in front of a screen with nothing substantial to show for it. It comes down to simple logistics in the end. These forms of entertainment consume too much time to allow us to indulge in them if we're trying in earnest to increase the range of our accomplishments. In the long run, what is more important? Is it better to pursue your dreams and keep to your schedule, or set your life aside for the next installment of a comedy or crime drama? There's very little middle ground on this subject either, since one program tends to encourage us to watch the next and before we know it, the entire night has gotten past us.

Blocking off Time

A more difficult, but no less vital part to reclaiming lost time is the establishment of periods of time where you are free of interruptions. For the hour or two that you focus on your major goal, for example, you should silence your phone, refuse to check e-mail, and make it known to friends and family that you'll be unavailable. Unexpected and unneeded interruptions can drain time away far beyond what we imagine. Barring interruption from these pivotal times is important in that it ensures we're actually spending the time on a goal that we think we are. Conversely, we need to make an effort not to distract *ourselves*. If we sit down to make progress on a large project and are suddenly overwhelmed with the urge to call a friend or write an e-mail to someone, we're losing the time that we afforded ourselves to complete the task.

There are other things that can be avoided more easily. Years ago, fast food held massive appeal to a large percentage of the population because it was a great "time saver." In modern society, however, with microwaves and readily-made foods of high quality, these restaurants pale in comparison to newer conveniences, and can scarcely be called "fast" at all. Their personal service has declined significantly in the past fifteen years as a result of various economic pressures, and it is actually far more likely that you are capable of feeding yourself in a fraction of the time it would take the average fast-food restaurant to bring your food to you. Again, minutes saved here and there add up through any given day, and a person determined to make the most of every day should be prepared to make changes to one's habits accordingly. Even those who cannot cook will find healthier and better-tasting meals available to them for lower prices.

Try to cook whenever possible. Keep your ingredients simple (no more than five per meal is generally a good rule of thumb) to keep the time spent on making your food to a minimum. Simple meals such as these are shown to drastically improve health and well-being, which will greatly assist you in staying motivated.

Doubling Up and Grouping Tasks

In this same vein, begin to search for ways of doubling up on tasks. Reading can be difficult to fit into one's schedule. Try getting used to it on a bike or treadmill if exercise is another habit you want to incorporate. If you commute to work, switch some of what you want to read into audiobook format and eliminate talk radio. When you start combining tasks in this fashion, you will be better able to come up with viable combinations for yourself. Simple tasks that can be done in tandem should be done so as much as possible. It's a good idea to make this sort of thing a game if you can—trying to compress one's daily affairs as much as possible will otherwise become a stressful experience for you, and possibly those around you. In other words, some people swear that brushing their teeth in the shower saves time, but it's hard to imagine that shaving while doing any other activity is realistic or safe—the same goes for applying make-up while driving. Don't engage in any activity that puts your welfare at risk. Combining tasks should be simple and easy to do. If the added concentration results in a significant deficit in one or both tasks, try a different combination.

Group similar tasks together in your schedule. It's all too easy to make a quick trip to the grocery store and return to complete your daily chores, only to realize that you also meant to make a quick trip to a different store. Again, this is where writing down a schedule comes in very handy. You're far more likely to remember everything you set out to accomplish when you get into your car if you have a written reminder with you at all times. If you've done that, all you need to do is glance at the list and check off whatever you've accomplished as you go. Without the list, the odds of forgetting something increases through frustration while you're stuck at the eighth red-light in a row. When this happens, we might skip a task, and once we get home, we're almost certainly not going back out again.

Motivation is Key to Productivity

The attentive reader may already notice a trend present in each of these habit-changing activities: motivation and persistence are essential if any change is to succeed. This is really just as common here as it is for any other task. By itself, motivation can be quite a difficult skill to acquire—at least on the outset. Staying motivated to remain productive can represent the largest challenge to actually being productive, especially since the practice is constantly being hindered by situations and circumstances beyond our control. Many of us will resolve to clean and wash our cars one weekend, and suddenly find ourselves or a family member struck down with a cold or flu. While such an occurrence certainly warrants our immediate attention, and we are right to delay other activities until the situation is resolved, we nevertheless feel vaguely defeated and discouraged.

For this reason, it is just as important for us to be forgiving of such circumstances. Acknowledgement and adherence to a set of rules regarding our own personal "guilt machines" is certainly in order, since we will inevitably suffer setbacks related to ingrained laziness or unforeseen events. When this happens, we can't let that knee-jerk reaction of guilt or apathy derail us further by causing us to avoid our tasks. Below are several things to remember when developing habits of increased personal productivity.

You're trying. That's not anything to balk at. You're making an effort to become more productive. Say, for instance, you write down a schedule for yourself, but awaken the next day and either forget it or cannot bring yourself to complete some of the very first tasks (we'll get into combating morning-moods later). Remember the difference between optimists and pessimists? Here, the pessimist comes home at the end of the day, sees the list, and grows overwhelmed with guilt at what he perceives to be the failure of completion. The optimist sees the list and thinks, "I wasn't able to do the things on my list today, but I wrote out my schedule, and that's better than nothing." The optimist will proceed to examine the list and determine what should happen next in order to make the schedule a success.

Motivation in the Morning

Many of us go to sleep with the best intentions for the next morning. We plan to wake up early and start the day off without a hitch. Upon beginning to write out schedules designed to enhance our personal productivity, we'll resolve to get up an hour earlier and get a head-start on all of the things we need to do. But in the morning, six or seven o'clock rolls around and as the alarm begins to blare, we suddenly lose interest. Perhaps you're thinking it's time to get up and go for a jog, but you're imagining it and lose all interest in doing so. If this is the case, it will benefit you greatly if you stop imagining the run or other unpleasant activity that you have planned. Like you've done with your major goals or big dreams, break the task down. What's the first thing you need to do in order to get out of bed and start your day?

The answer is: get moving. Sit up if you can. If you can't, move your arms or legs until you're ready to sit up. If you can't move your arms or legs, wiggle your fingers or toes—anything to try and increase circulation. Take deep breaths, get oxygen to your brain, and work towards sitting up and eventually getting out of bed. This is no small task—especially on nights when we've stayed up longer than we should. Nonetheless, a life of increased personal productivity is lacking a key advantage if our mornings don't begin early enough.

Once you're out of bed, and again especially if you've had somewhat less sleep than you should have, it's likely you'll be combating morning stiffness. The most effective way to fight this off is more stretching, especially your upper and lower back. This is a good time to begin exercising. It may seem or feel like a ludicrous proposition first thing in the morning, but it is common knowledge amongst morning joggers that such physical activity in the morning can benefit one throughout the entire day in a wide range of ways. If you try it, remember to stretch and perhaps walk a little first, but you're morning-sluggishness will dissolve in a matter of minutes for certain.

It might seem counterintuitive to try and develop new habits first thing in the morning—but this is actually the best possible time there is for doing so. Our mental acuity in the AM far surpasses that in the evening—once we get over the grogginess, that is. We are more likely to complete tasks we've committed to before the demands of the day set in and we find our resolve flagging.

Getting to Sleep Quickly

As difficult at times as it is for us to wake up in the morning, it can be equally difficult for us to go to sleep at night. This is especially true if we aren't much for physical activity or something is weighing on our minds. A steady sleep schedule is vital to productivity; a person who tries to go to sleep at ten but lies awake for an hour or two has lost both that time to himself for the evening and is likely to suffer a similar loss in the morning. Many of us commit to lying down and waiting for sleep to set in—but if sleep fails to come to within twenty minutes of lying down, it's a good idea to get off of the bed and engage in some mild activity. Don't watch TV in order to fall asleep though—instead, listen to music, read, or clean something that can be easily cleaned. After you've done this, try to sleep again. By doing this, you are trying to get your body out of the habit of lying awake in your bed—which it may unconsciously be accustomed to if it takes you a while to fall asleep at night.

Breaking that habit will do wonders for both your health and your productivity. By this same token, taking on what you perceive as your most unpleasant task the very first thing in the morning will make it more likely that you actually do it. If you get the hardest part of your day out of the way before anything else, then you've taken a big step towards defeating procrastination in general. Wake up, power through it, and everything else is easier than the first thing you did.

Get Accountability from a Friend

For many activities that you wish to do during the day, consider "buddying up." Finding a friend who is like-minded can increase your motivation, allow you to discuss common hindrances you've been facing, and provide additional resources for overcoming obstacles along the way. Here, the selection of your so-called accountability buddy is critical, and will need to be tailored to suit your personality. Some of us simply need to vent about a given problem before we can proceed. To a person of this nature, a friend who simply offers solutions rather than providing emotional support may not be of much use. On the other hand, for those of us accustomed to restricting emotional expression and instead focus on solutions, it would be a far better fit to buddy up with someone with a detached view of the situation. This friend can often provide an unforeseen solution to the problem. Most of us will fall somewhere in the middle of either extreme—and you will notice as you progress that you may seek actual solutions for some specific tasks and emotional resonance for others.

This friend will be a person you can discuss goals and progress with openly, whatever the case may be. Often times, talking through situations and scenarios with another person provides that extra impetus just when we need it—and friends who hold similar aspirations to you are excellent sources of encouragement and support. This is true especially when we would otherwise find ourselves floundering for want of constructive dialogue. This will come in handy if the activity or hobby you wish to develop can be done by several people at once—to that end, be sure to take advantage of community resources for activities you're interested in pursuing.

Power Through It

Another strategy for picking up the productivity when you feel yourself slowing or becoming tired is to simply power through it. Often times we're misled when we feel like exhaustion is causing us to fail to complete tasks as well as we should. It likely will not surprise you to learn that an overwhelming amount of energy you expend towards the completion of almost anything will be dedicated to the very last details of whatever task you've undertaken. While this might seem like tedium, it's important to make a conscious effort to reframe this phenomenon as something like an illusion.

Our brains are much better at summing up and providing a range of estimates for simpler tasks with fewer steps. When an accomplishment contains several stages, we're far more likely to misappropriate the amount of time it will take to complete the task overall. We'll leave out a step in our planning or not realize that additional stages may be necessary. Thus, as we proceed, we may find ourselves flagging as our thoughts begin to assess how much more time something has taken than we originally thought it would.

For projects with no other value than our own sense of personal accomplishment, this can have two outcomes. First, since no one is depending on the task's completion except for you, you likely won't feel a sense of dread or anxiety (though frustration is common enough in these situations). Unfortunately, anxieties brought about by deadlines are highly motivating. We may be able to shake a goal off by telling ourselves that we don't feel like doing it, but try having a similar conversation with your boss at work and you'll see the difference. Without this external force to drive us toward the completion of a task, we're at somewhat of a loss to find reasons to continue. In this case, we simply need to pick up our spirits and move on with the task at hand—if, that is, we determine that our sense of self-worth is valuable enough, and it is always valuable enough.

Just going for it is easier said than done, or you wouldn't be reading this book in the first place. Easy enough to say it, but *how*? Perhaps you've even read books on the subject of motivation, and they can give you helpful pointers that might help you every now and then. However, more often than not, much of the literature on the subject can miss a very simple and very significant fact about motivation. The truth is, it isn't the rational thinking centers in our brain that have a major impact on our motivation. We aren't driven to do things that we think about regularly; we are driven to do things we *feel* strongly about.

Motivation is not a logical process—it is an emotional one. It is the development of new emotional outlooks, not rational understanding, that will push us forward. We're not teaching ourselves new ways of thinking—at least, the work doesn't stop there. Instead, what we need to do in order to become more productive is to change the ways in which we *feel*. Unfortunately, many works in self-development emphasize the cognitive thinking processes rather than the emotive or motivational affectations they are designed to. Changing the way you think isn't a bad idea by any means if the outcome is to increase motivation; but if a thought-process you've adopted or are trying to incorporate isn't working, it's time to move onto something else and see if that works.

Below are some common tips and thought exercises designed to tap into your emotional power.

If you find yourself writing up a schedule every night but simply tossing it aside every morning, practice any of these techniques until you've found something that works for you. The reaction you'll be looking for will be one of sudden clarity and direction. If, for example, you decide to imagine yourself successful and fulfilled after the task is completed, your visualization will take on a vivid texture and you'll notice your heart-rate rise suddenly with enthusiasm. It's not enough to know what you should do and understand why you should do it—you have to *feel* it.

Avoid Exhaustion - Make Sure It's Doable

This sounds obvious, but when faced with a task and a sudden motivational impetus, we tend to set our sights far too high above what we can actually accomplish in the time we've allotted ourselves. Goals should always be broken down into discrete pieces that can be accomplished simply and within an hour or two. Deciding to work on a massive project for six hours at a time may *seem* like the best way to tackle it at first, but after the first several hundred minutes, we may find ourselves exhausted. In this case, it's a much better idea to take a break and resolve to come back to the task at a later time, when we are restored and possess a fresher perspective. Two hours of solid work on a project is better than spending six hours where more and more of your time is simply spent trying to push forward. If you're constantly setting up huge amounts of time for yourself and finding that you run out of time or energy quickly, you can become easily discouraged. Set up tasks for yourself where you are bound to succeed at first.

Completion-Imaging

This can be a good exercise to reinvigorate yourself midway through a task, or to bring yourself to begin something you've been putting off for a while. Close your eyes and use your imagination to visualize the task being absolutely finished. Try to give the mental image as much vivid detail as you possibly can, paying attention to the way you feel. Let yourself feel as excited as you can—don't pay attention to the fact that it's just in your imagination. Instead, use that energy—the imagined enthusiasm at having finished something difficult—and imagine yourself starting that task with the very same enthusiasm.

There's a minor distinction here that becomes important in the application of this procedure. If you simply picture yourself as being enthusiastic, but don't feel any of that enthusiasm directly, you might not be able to access that emotion as well as you'll need to. If this is the case, instead of viewing the scenario in the first person, imagine yourself somewhat distanced from it—perhaps ten feet away. While you remain emotionally detached, watch yourself becoming more and more enthusiastic about the task as though you were watching a movie. Take as long as you feel appropriate, then simply move your awareness into the mental image you've created of yourself.

Feel your thoughts merging with the visualization, and feel the visualization's emotional processes take over your own—leaving you driven and directed toward the task at hand. You'll find quickly that this is a better jump-start to your motivation for bigger tasks. Menial tasks such as chores or errands may benefit more from later exercises. This represents a basic attempt at trying to access emotions which would drive you towards a larger goal by focusing on positive end results. You can then utilize the potential benefits of increased productivity to your advantage.

Identify Your Strengths and Weaknesses

Come up with a list of things you consider yourself to be good at, and things that you feel you still need to work on. You might be a good organizer, or great at remaining clutter-free. Perhaps you're a skilled persuader, or able to understand others' points of view more readily than those around you. Do you have a knack for attention to detail? Perhaps you're better at big-picture situations, or good at being able to identify potential pitfalls and avoid them.

It's good to know your strengths, but even better to know what sorts of things you'd like to work on. If, for example, you feel you are a poor communicator, being a better one can easily become a goal for you. If you tend to collect disorganization, make it a point to practice cutting down on the amount of clutter or mess you make for several hours a week. There's no rule anywhere that says you have to adhere to a bad habit just because you've done so in the past—that is to say, just because you do something you don't like, that doesn't mean it's a part of your personality. We're all capable of learning new skills and incorporating them into our daily lives, with sufficient motivation.

Remind Yourself of Past Successes

If you find your energy dropping due to lack of confidence or fear of failure, take a minute or two to recall something which you succeeded at. This will be most helpful to you if you can recall something similar to what you are currently attempting to accomplish. Mull it over and try to remember your thoughts and mindset before you were successful. Oftentimes, you'll discover that your way of thinking was similar then to what it is now. In this way, we can steady ourselves and move forward with whatever we need to get done.

Conversely, any time you are successful with a task, make note of it and take pride. You've just acquired another model of behavior that will help you in the future with similar tasks. You've made it that much easier for yourself when the next time comes around to accomplish a related objective. Be sure to ask yourself what made you accomplish the goal. If the answer is something like "I knew I had to do it, so I just went ahead and did it," you're onto something!

Remind yourself constantly of the things that you are good at. Draw whatever you can from your strengths. If, for example, you consider yourself a poor speaker, but have often earned praise for your ability to write clearly and concisely, consider writing out things you might need to say in phone conversations or meetings in person. You may not actually need to read directly from your list, but the notes will help spur you along in the direction you wish to go.

Music is a Simple Distraction Preventer

This is good for menial chores, where your mind could be clamoring for something a bit more stimulating than the task at hand. Music or audiobooks are also a great replacement for watching TV or movies during the evening—they aren't as distracting as visual media, so you'll be far less likely to lose minutes (or hours) here and there while you're trying to accomplish something.

Choose whatever you like. Certain music may suit some chores better than others for you. Find what works. Consider using headphones, for two reasons. First, this will ensure you're not bothering anyone else in your household. Second, it will keep interruptions less likely to interfere with your productivity—a silenced cell-phone can still buzz, after all. Try to stay away from the radio, however. The ads and talk over the air can be surprisingly distracting when you've just determined to accomplish something important to you.

Monitoring Your Progress

For those of you with a penchant for analyzing your progress, charting and graphing programs like Microsoft Excel can have incredible motivational power. You'll need a basic understanding of how to convert the table information into a graph, and you might want to check your progress on a daily or weekly basis. You can set an "average" amount of goals you want to complete every day, perhaps dividing them up into minor, moderate, and major ones. Be sure to try to give yourself room for improvement. You can even transfer your written schedule into an Excel chart. This has the added advantage of keeping both of your progress logs in one place, since you can annotate the cells to your heart's content. Keeping a careful record of your progress really is an excellent way to stay motivated. One of the reasons that graphs and charts are a must for business presentations and the like is that they put whatever goals your company is discussing into concrete visual layouts. You have every reason to expect that the more detailed and visually aided your own attempts at progress are, the farther you will get.

The nature of the graph itself is really up to you—as stated above, consider dividing your tasks into minor, moderate, and major goals. At the end of every day, take stock of what you've completed against what you didn't. Give yourself a set of points for each task, depending on how important it was to complete it—for example, use "one" for minor, "three" for moderate, and "five" for major tasks.

Keep a tally of these points across time if it helps. You can check yourself against your average in this fashion. In this way, you'll also be able to establish a somewhat more objective baseline for your productivity. You'll know when you're really moving, so to speak, and when you're going slowly. Also be sure to mark times on your chart when you were disrupted, since it will help you identify times that interruptions are common in order to avoid them in the future. Mark when you are sick, when a task unexpectedly comes up, and so on. This way, you'll know when you have reasons for why you were unable to complete the tasks versus when you were not sufficiently motivated toward them.

Be prepared to hold onto these charts and graphs. It may sound silly, but think of them as a record of your own progress. Months and years from now, you can look back at your earlier attempts at productivity and physically see what you've accomplished since then. This is especially useful if we feel we've fallen into some kind of rut—nothing will motivate you more in the present than suddenly remembering you've done similar (or even more difficult) tasks a month or two ago. You might even rediscover a way of partitioning up a task you're on the road to completing by taking a look at sufficient data from past experiences.

Keeping track of productivity in this fashion also serves as a testament to your commitment to stay on whatever path you've chosen. Think of it like an ever-growing trophy that reflects your accomplishments in time and energy well-spent. You'll be far more motivated to forgo your daily television or internet regimen if you do so.

Rewarding Yourself

This is an especially good motivator if the hobby or goals you've engaged in can earn you money on the side. If you're increasing your income by crafting, internet services, or anything else, set a monetary goal, and agree to reward yourself with something you will *really* enjoy once you've obtained that goal. Whatever you decide to reward yourself with, make sure it doesn't exceed the money you've taken in by completing your goals. Other than that, anything is fair game. If possible, you can even reward yourself with something that will benefit the craft you practice. Say, for instance, that you've developed a passion for photography. Why not reward yourself with a better camera, lens, or flash once you've reached five-hundred dollars, or whatever figure suits you?

B.F. Skinner, the founder of what is currently known as Behavioral Science, identified motivators that encouraged all kinds of behaviors. While he identified them in animals such as mice and pigeons, much of what he discovered can be applied in order to modify human behavior. If you complete a task, and are immediately rewarded for the completion of that task, you will be more motivated toward that behavior in the future. Skinner generally used food, but here's where the advantage of being human comes in: we have a wide range of objects and activities that can reinforce our behavior.

To some extent, this is why television and movies are so popular. All you need to do is turn the box on, and it provides you with as much entertainment as you want. Unfortunately, as we've already discussed, this activity drastically reduces our productivity and leads to long-term complications over time. The trick here is to establish a scheduled set of reinforcement and stick with it. Be careful not to reward yourself for something as simple as logging onto your computer or checking your correspondence with hours of wasted time. Alternatives are abundant, so think of things that you enjoy doing outside the realm of passive media and stick with those.

There are certainly worse ways to spend extra income than rewarding your dedicated effort, and it's always a good idea to foster a skill in some way that will grant monetary benefits. The money itself will prove to be a powerful reinforcement for your continued perseverance. Another important aspect of behaviorism, especially in humans, is that after a while the task itself becomes reinforcing, since it has been paired with such desirable outcomes.

Make Yourself a Workspace

You'll need a place to complete whatever you've set out to complete. This is especially important if you tend to read in the same place that you write, or relax in the same place that you work. We're surprisingly susceptible to "locational cues," and this can lead us to become suddenly distracted with a task if the place we've chosen to do it in is somewhere we're not accustomed to being productive. Give yourself an office space. This will be a room if possible, but it could also simply be a corner in your home that sees less traffic than other places. Wherever this workspace is, make it as free of distractions as possible—don't put a bookshelf loaded with fiction next to the computer desk you've set aside for blogging or graphic design, for example. You may suddenly find yourself distracted while flipping through a book you enjoy when you are set to work.

Find inspirational phrases (or better yet, come up with your own) to decorate your work area with. If you're an artist, decorate the area with your best work, or work from others that inspires you to create. Find anything that will motivate you to keep moving, and don't be afraid to change things up. If you find yourself unmotivated by something in your workspace, feel free to discard it and replace it with something that will help you. But don't let these little motivators pile up. Keep this workplace as clutter-free as possible. When disorder piles up, our motivation to accomplish goes down. Your workspace should consist of as much organization as possible. It should be as simple and as spare as you can make it. If something doesn't belong in your work area, move it somewhere else.

Schedule Relaxation

You won't be able to work every day nonstop, and indeed, why should you? It's important to find the right balance between productivity and time that you spend unwinding and reflecting on what you've managed to accomplish. Try to schedule an hour or two when you can switch gears and take it easy. If you have family, engage with them in some meaningful way. Walk your dog. Read from a book.

Phone a friend or family member you haven't spoken to in a while.

Do take time to consider what activities (aside from television) genuinely relax you. It's also a good idea to use some of this time for power-naps. Fifteen minutes or so spent generally relaxing and thinking things over can get things moving for you again when you're ready to resume your productivity.

Get Your Spouse or Family Motivated

Odds are, if you are married, you share hobbies or desires in common with your spouse. Incorporating them into your activities is a great way to establish support and tackle larger goals. If you're interested in further increasing your productivity with respect to a certain goal, and your spouse has expressed interest in the same thing, it's a great idea to try and incorporate them into your plans. Make it a team activity—two people can accomplish far more than either individually.

Taking this a step further, consider what your children do chore-wise around the house. If they're old enough, it might be time to start your son or daughter washing dishes, vacuuming, or making sure the yard is properly watered. Delegating these sorts of chores can free up lots of time. If you're thinking *"easier said than done,"* you're absolutely right! As adults, we tend to forget how children process the things around them. It's very common for parents to simply tell a child to clean their room because they need to. If the child asks *why* they need to, the parent often responds *because it simply needs to be done.*

As true as this might be, it's completely beside the point for all but the most diligent and eager-to-please sons and daughters around. And really, this kind of circular reasoning is never why we do things in the first place. If we were motivated to do things just because they needed to be done, we wouldn't need to work on finding new reasons to motivate ourselves in the first place. Taken into account that a child doesn't have anywhere near the life experience of an adult, is it really rational for us to expect them to suddenly commit to tasks that have no intrinsic value to them?

To this end, it will be beneficial to come up with a reward schedule for your child. If they perform tasks, they get something in return—an allowance or even a gift card for Amazon or iTunes. Rewards will work best if they are frequent, but they should be small and immediate. If you're struggling to get your son or daughter to do a decent job sweeping the driveway, and suddenly they do a good job, make sure that they know it. It's far too common that we say something along the lines of "that's what you should have done in the first place." Eliciting that kind of attitude towards the successful accomplishment of a task will reduce the likelihood that the success will occur in the future. Always try to avoid being negative in your appraisal of chore completions. That's like punishing someone for trying to do something they probably didn't want to do in the first place.

When you run errands, involve your children in some way in order to save time. For example, on a trip to the grocery store, have lists prepared for them and set them out towards finding items—if they are old enough, of course! Try to allocate as much responsibility as your child's age will allow. This will take patience if they are accustomed to their parents handling all the chores around the house, but it will be worth it in the long run.

Other Methods to Get More Done

Decide Quickly

Have you ever reached a point in a task where you come to an unexpected decision? It's common when presented with an unexpected problem or choice to stop work and mull it over. However, such mulling can lead to long-term delays in the completion of a task. When you come to such places, give yourself a definite amount of time to make a decision—say, twenty seconds to a full minute. Once you've made that decision, act on it and proceed with whatever you were doing. This helps avoid tying unnecessary time up in coming to a decision that you're actually just as capable of making in the moment.

Feeling this need to stop is akin to procrastination. Suddenly, we're not as certain how to proceed so we feel the need to stop until something external clicks into place and we can continue. But the decision is always *ours to make*, and we are best benefited by deciding quickly and moving on. You'll often find that you can begin to make these types of decisions almost immediately. You already know what you're trying to accomplish, and whatever decision you make in the instant will reflect that knowledge. If you go with your intuition, you'll generally be right.

Do a Horrible Job

Some people swear by this method. When faced with a task that provokes extreme anxiety in you, don't set out to do your best at first. Instead, do it as poorly as you can. Make fun of the task and how nervous you are at completing it. Go for it. Just know that no one will ever see what you're doing, so it won't matter. Once you've finished, you can set out to complete the task in a more serious manner. You'll be surprised at how much of what you thought was terrible actually becomes the foundation for what you accomplish. After all, if you've done an intentionally bad job, you can only improve on it from there. Review any task you've completed and see if it's really as bad as you thought—you'll often find that you've given yourself an important foundation for whatever goal you've made for yourself. Give yourself a license to make light of the task, and the completion of it may suddenly become tangible and achievable.

This is a great way to defeat the more threatening aspects of major goals, and is really akin to a form of game play. In a sense, you're still accomplishing the task you set out to achieve for yourself. Since it is for yourself, you don't need to worry about failure—especially since you set out with failure in mind. Intentionally making a mess of something you want to accomplish can rearrange it for you in a way that takes the stress out of a situation.

Always Educate Yourself

There are books, courses, and materials available for just about everything you could possibly want to achieve. Again, sites like Amazon.com and Half.com become incredibly useful. Log on, type in the skill or hobby you're trying to cultivate, and search the results. Very likely, you won't need to go past the first page to come up with something that can help with your specific goal. There may even be classes or groups in your area dedicated to the same idea, and joining them will greatly increase your productivity and provide a very useful burst of motivation. You'll find answers to questions, simple directions to seemingly complicated problems, emotional support, and further suggestions for reading or developing your goals.

This is where devices like e-readers and tablets can again come in extremely handy. Why order a book for delivery (and have it take up just that much more space when it arrives) if you can pay less for the book, nothing at all for shipping, and receive it immediately? The electronic reading revolution is still under development, but nearly any book you can buy will be cheaper in an e-format. Oftentimes, the difference can result in long-term savings of hundreds of dollars.

However you decide to build up your academic materials for the pursuits of your choice, take books one at a time. Books often make references to other books, and it's a good idea to keep yet another list of materials you may need in the future. Do be sure to finish reading (and taking notes) from one book at a time—it's always important to keep your attention directed to one aspect of a goal at a time. Once you've finished it, go back and look at your notes. Use your intuition to tell you what you need more information on next, and look for something on that subject.

You can also find an endless supply of podcasts and other electronic materials on sites like YouTube.com, and these are just clicks away from being a part of your knowledge. Many such books come out with regular updates or have associated websites and blogs attached to them. These sites can contain additional tips and pointers for anything you may wish to accomplish; while the purchase of the book it supplements may be optimal for your productivity, it is by no means necessary if the price is higher than you'd prefer.

This is also a good way to make use of your commute, if you spend a considerable amount of time going to and from work every day. Instead of talk radio, find these same materials in audio format and listen to them that way. The more you immerse yourself in the goals you've set out to accomplish, the more likely you'll be to follow through with them. This is especially useful for major goals, and people in search of success stories. You'll be surprised at how similar they are to yours at the outset. If that's true, why can't their story ultimately be yours in the end?

Get Up, Do Something Else

We often get trapped in particular modes of thought. When this happens, it's often a good idea to engage in activities that don't obviously relate to our goals. This can change up our way of dealing with particular problems and provide critical moments of inspiration. If your goal leaves you sitting at a desk for hours on end and you find yourself coming up against an inordinate amount of mental obstacles, it's time to change your environment. You can do something as simple as going for a walk, or you can take up a completely separate hobby with no specific goals in mind. Let your mind drift back to your main goal occasionally and write down any thoughts you might have on the subject. To this end, keep a notebook and pen with you while you engage in this secondary task. Many important insights are lost simply because they were not recorded at the time of inspiration.

Physical activity works best for a secondary goal—this is yet another reason why physical exercise is so important. It's common knowledge now that physical activity can increase mental productivity, and when you're feeling sluggish, nothing will help you more than a quick swim or jog to break up the monotony. Naturally, if you do choose to swim, you won't be able to keep your pen and notebook directly on you, but keep it nearby. If something occurs to you regarding your main goal, direct yourself immediately to record it.

The Myth of Multitasking

This form of task management involves the completion of two (or perhaps three) objectives that can be completed simultaneously. This will almost guarantee that either task is completed more slowly than it would be on its own. But for menial tasks that do not require dedicated effort, multitasking can allow you to complete two tasks in less time than if you'd done them one after the other.

The idea of multitasking on significant goals may seem appealing, but it's important to know that research throughout the 1990s on the concept revealed that it is **not** a good method to adopt when tackling larger projects. Anything that requires a modicum of planning or preparation is not a good candidate for simultaneous completion with another. For instance, trying to have a phone conversation while designing a new piece of furniture will have you distracted and unable to focus on either task. It's important to understand our psychological limitations regarding multi-tasking so that we don't try to double up on things that will require our direct attention. Doing so will waste time and resources that would be better spent directed at one project at a time.

That being said, there are things we can do simultaneously with little loss to either task. As stated above, listening to books on audio format is a great way to spend your time in transit (though this represents the absolute limits of activities you should engage in while driving). You can also feel free to spend your lunch and breakfast eating while directing your attention to tasks that involve planning and mental preparation. If you've decided to take up knitting, you might reach a point where a phone conversation is manageable while doing so.

Failures and Delays – Don't Let Them Get to You

Don't let failures, delays, or just plain misfortune get to you. Admittedly, the practice of shaking off bad luck or speed-bumps along that way is difficult. Each of us inherently knows that we're capable of more than we are presently accomplishing. When we encounter things that are simply beyond our control, we can quickly leap to an emotional conclusion that it was somehow our fault the task was not completed on time. If something goes wrong, look at why it may have gone wrong and try to distance it from your sense of self-worth. Look at the situation as objectively as possible and run it by someone you trust, if necessary.

We believe we're capable of more than we presently accomplish because *we are*. When things get in the way, allow yourself to accept a temporary setback without succumbing to feelings of total failure. Things do happen on a regular basis that will necessarily distract us from our goals. It's important to stay committed to these goals and ensure that they are only frustrated in the moment.

It's a good practice to keep trying and working through problems precisely when these feelings seem like they are about to overwhelm you. We have a tendency to anchor ourselves in previous expectations. For an easy example, try walking across a surface six inches wide, raised just a few feet off the ground. If this sounds doable, that's because it would be an easy accomplishment for almost anyone. Take that same plank, however, and set it between to rooftops several hundred feet in the air, and suddenly the possibility of failure seems much greater, even if we haven't changed the actual task.

Much of our behavior is the result of acting on previous beliefs and assumptions, and a simple change in those assumptions can lead to progress. It was long thought that no airplane could ever surpass the speed of sound—researchers insisted that the resonating stress involved in such great velocities would tear anything apart. In fact, however, the first plane to break the sound barrier suddenly stopped shuddering and travelled far smoother than it had under the barrier. Likewise, experts thought that a human being could never run anything faster than a four minute mile. Several decades ago, when this barrier was broken, the feat was suddenly repeated hundreds of times over in a short period of time. In the 1960s and 70s, leading computer industry experts found the idea of people having machines in their homes downright laughable.

Negative and positive emotions are both affected by this type of anchoring. This is great for positive emotions, since they naturally direct us toward what we want in life. For negative emotions, however, they can only hold us back, and that means these beliefs are harmful to our productivity. No change will be immediate—you'll likely feel frustrated by many of your goals in time—but gradual change is inevitable in the face of constant attempts made to do so. Whatever your personal setbacks may be, recognize that you are trying to move forward, and in trying, you are slowly succeeding—even if that feeling of success isn't always accessible.

The ancient Greeks told the story of Orpheus, who descended into the underworld to retrieve his beloved Eurydice. Hades agreed to release her, on the grounds that Orpheus would not turn around to see if her spirit was actually following him on his way out. Orpheus traveled the entire distance back to the above world without glancing behind him, until he reached the cavern exit and was plagued by a terrible doubt. He hadn't seen or heard Eurydice since he began his journey. He believed he had been duped by Hades, and as he turned around, he saw the shade of his love fade back into the darkness, never to be seen again. Two more steps, *perhaps one*, and he would have achieved his goal.

Lucky for us, the Greeks were pessimistic in their appraisal of the human spirit. Whatever goals you have will not suddenly vanish into the darkness the moment you begin to doubt. They can, however, become unduly suspended by our disbelief. If we let these doubts prey on our motivations sufficiently, they can delay our accomplishments indefinitely, and that is a situation we should all strive to avoid. We do, after all, owe ourselves the full effort and attention required of our best and biggest dreams.

Moving Through the Tough Spots

As much as you should limit the ability negative emotions have on you from completing a task, you should be just as willing to continue with your goals in the face of whatever stress or anxieties you are experiencing. Recognize your fear of failure or success as such, and make an effort to finish your goal anyway.

The best way to begin this practice is by choosing small tasks that you hold little value for, but may nonetheless be completed. Tackle these little ones first, and move on to big ones once you know you can do it. Major tasks in life will always require greater effort and focus from us, and we're more likely to follow through with something if we ultimately feel confident that we can do it.

Declutter

The ability to stay organized and mess-free is a goal for many of us in and of itself. When junk tends to pile up around us, we're less likely to feel motivated. A clean workspace, on the other hand, can give us the impetus and mental focus we need in order to direct ourselves through almost anything. The more organized the tools of your trade, the faster you will be able to find anything you might need.

To this end, if you find clutter piling up about you, set to work on your belongings with large plastic bags. Find your nearest goodwill and start making trips. If something can't be used, throw it away or recycle it. Think about getting rid of objects you haven't used in a year or so; consider whether or not they really have enough sentimental value to hold onto. Chances are, you won't even notice that it's gone.

De-cluttering can become one of the minor goals you incorporate into your schedule. In fact, if you devote as little as ten minutes a day to this type organizational activity, results will accumulate quickly. Choose a room, and get to work on it. There will be no need to set specific objectives here. All you need to do is start getting rid of clutter in that particular area until it's gone. Simply set out to remove anything you don't need from the space. Be prepared to give it away if you can, and throw it away if the object is no longer usable. Attack closet spaces, cupboards and the like to free up the most space—that's where most of the unnecessary things wind up.

To prevent further clutter from invading your space while you're trying to take care of the problem, try to remove one or two pieces of clutter from your home for every new object that comes in. Take a look at your wardrobe—are there things in there you haven't worn in eight months, or perhaps a year? Take a look at your dishes, and see if any are chipped or cracked that can reasonably be thrown out. How many bottles of Windex or other cleaning supplies do you have in your house? Look at your bookshelf and determine if you'll ever read certain books again. The answer is almost certainly *no*, and they'll do more good donated to a public library than they will taking up space in your home. Productivity and organization go hand in hand, just as much as disorder and apathy do. By getting rid of anything that's unnecessary, you're helping yourself maintain a positive attitude.

Final Note

Motivation and productivity go hand in hand, as do dedication and organization. There's no way around the obstacles presently keeping you from your goals but *through* them. Efforts to increase personal productivity will be an ongoing process that causes you to evaluate and eliminate old and inefficient habits in order to replace them with new ones. Changing a habit is a major accomplishment, and should be rewarded as such. Succumbing to the old habits, however, must be expected. We won't be able to transform ourselves overnight into productivity-driven machines. Take great care not to beat yourself up mentally for minor slip-ups now and then. In fact, don't even take major slip-ups or perceived failures to heart. Doing so won't help you get where you're going. The only thing that can help you accomplish your goals is your own persistence and active attempts at striving forward.

When you set out towards a goal, don't expect the goal to get easier. Instead, expect your ability to achieve that goal to become stronger. Increasingly, your personal productivity is a testament to your character and ability to achieve. Taking interest in the information and resources discussed in this book proves that you are at the very least interested in doing so. *Now it's time to figure out how interested in it you really are.*

Develop your own personal style. For goal-setting and scheduling, are you a spiral-bound notebook sort of personality? Maybe you prefer word-processing programs on a computer, or binders that will easily allow you to rearrange information and notes on your progress. For your workspace, choose the style that fits you best. If you're motivated by visual images, do you prefer Escher or Rembrandt? If you find yourself collecting quotes on your subject matter, try to determine if you prefer humorous quips as opposed to spiritual musings or vice versa. This book can give you an outline of the procedures and techniques you can use to adjust your time-usage and hopefully provide tips at fostering emotional well-being in the process. In the end, though, it will be up to you to determine your own style.

Don't be afraid to get quirky—successful and productive types often are. This is because they are more comfortable with asserting themselves in the presence of adversity, and have grown far more accustomed to dealing with failures and setbacks. But, it is possible, given time and patience. Einstein once remarked to a student who was experiencing difficulty in the subject of mathematics that he should not worry, because Einstein's own difficulties in the subject were infinitely greater. Einstein himself had, prior to his sudden worldwide renown, suffered from extraordinary feelings of self-doubt and hopelessness. His entire life, his teachers, peers, and nearly everyone around him, had perceived him as unremarkable, uninteresting, and below average.

Most of us would be happy to change the world to a mere fraction of the degree accomplished by Einstein. We can take his statement about his difficulty in mathematics and apply it to anything we wish to achieve in life. Whatever we set out to do, there is likely already someone who has faced our very same challenge with even more doubt and uncertainty, and accomplished it nonetheless.

Also by Justin Byers:

The Stress Free Work Day - How to Effectively Organize Your Day, Be Super Productive, Increase Your Motivation, and Get Out By 5! – Justin Byers

Related Books You Will Enjoy

The Stress Free You: How to Live Stress Free and Feel Great Everyday, Starting Today – Elizabeth O'Brien

The Problem is YOU: How to Get Out of Your Own Way and Conquer Self-Defeating Behavior – John Burke

Be Happy! - How to Stop Negative Thinking, Start Focusing on the Positive, and Create Your Happiness Mindset – Nicole Fisher

How to Quiet Your Mind: Relax and Silence the Voice of Your Mind Today! - A Beginner's Guide – Marc Allen

Visit EmpowermentNation.com to view these books and more!

**Visit
EmpowermentNation.com
to view other fantastic books,
sign up for book alerts, giveaways, and
updates!**